On Shakespeare's Sonnets

RELATED TITLES

Shakespeare's Sonnets, Revised Edition,
edited by Katherine Duncan-Jones
Arden Shakespeare Third Series

On
Shakespeare's
Sonnets

A Poets' Celebration

Edited by
Hannah Crawforth and
Elizabeth Scott-Baumann

Bloomsbury Arden Shakespeare
An imprint of Bloomsbury Publishing Plc

B L O O M S B U R Y
LONDON · OXFORD · NEW YORK · NEW DELHI · SYDNEY

Bloomsbury Arden Shakespeare

An imprint of Bloomsbury Publishing Plc

Imprint previously known as Arden Shakespeare

50 Bedford Square	1385 Broadway
London	New York
WC1B 3DP	NY 10018
UK	USA

www.bloomsbury.com

BLOOMSBURY, THE ARDEN SHAKESPEARE and the Diana logo are trademarks of Bloomsbury Publishing Plc

First published 2016

Editorial matter, selection and preface © Hannah Crawforth and Elizabeth Scott-Baumann, 2016
Each poem © its named author, 2016
Foreword © Colin Thubron, 2016

British Library Cataloguing-in-Publication Data
A catalogue record for this book is available from the British Library.

ISBN: HB: 978-1-4742-2158-0

Library of Congress Cataloging-in-Publication Data
A catalog record for this book is available from the Library of Congress.

Typeset by Fakenham Prepress Solutions, Fakenham, Norfolk, NR21 8NN
Printed and bound in India

Contents

Foreword

Time and again in his sonnets, Shakespeare asserts the immortality of his verse. Flesh and flowers will perish, stone and brass will be destroyed, but 'my verse shall stand'. His claim has proved prophetic. More than four hundred years after their publication, they live on.

They live on in the form in which Shakespeare wrote them: we read, memorize, quote, ponder them. But they also survive in the writing of others. Their influence endures in sonnets from Milton to Keats to John Berryman; in novels from Wilde's *Dorian Gray* to Woolf's *Orlando* to Burgess's *Nothing Like the Sun*; in criticism by Eliot, Spender, Auden. It is to this tradition that the poems in *On Shakespeare's Sonnets* belong. They have found their inspiration in a meter, an image, a mood, a turn of phrase, to become something of their own.

The poets in this collection, among the most distinguished in the language, have here been released into their own idioms of irony, passion and playfulness, which sometimes break out from the sonnet form that generated them. Their subjects, while perhaps addressed to a beloved, are multitudinous, and often subversive of formal expectation: a subversion in tune with the poet who is their stimulus. For Shakespeare's own two poetic loves – a beautiful youth and a promiscuous woman – were, by Petrarchan standards, hardly conventional.

The dense complexity of Shakespeare's sonnets is rarely attempted here. Four centuries have transformed poetic form and technique. But in them, time's passage remains inexorable, and the nuances of fulfilled or unrequited love still hold centre stage. The sonnets' confidence in poetic immortality – that 'eyes not yet created' will forever read these words – is seldom stressed: a by-product, perhaps, of our age of foreboding. But the value vested in words is here freshly affirmed by the care taken with them, by their precision and beauty, and by their vibrant refashioning of thought and emotion.

Colin Thubron
Royal Society of Literature

Preface

William Shakespeare died on 23 April 1616, which may have been his birthday. That his life should seemingly end on the anniversary of the day it began is apt, for Shakespeare's death represents the start of a long and vibrant afterlife for the poet's works. Shakespeare's plays and poems have continued to be read and performed around the world, translated into every language imaginable, and reinterpreted in every possible way. This book seeks to continue the tradition of reinventing Shakespeare, while also serving to commemorate his writing in the year of the quatercentenary of his death. In collaboration with the Royal Society of Literature we invited thirty of their fellows, some of the best poets working in English today, to respond to Shakespeare's sonnets in their own form, voice and style. The poems they produced appear here alongside the sonnets with which they engage most closely. At times this engagement is detailed and sustained; at others a single word, phrase, metaphor or fleeting feeling prompted their imaginations to take flight (an image our cover design evokes). In all instances it is Shakespeare's language, his verbal brilliance, the dazzling way that he crystallizes all of human life into a poetic instant, which our poets respond to here.

While such virtuosic qualities are on display throughout his works, they are perhaps most potently captured in his sonnets; 154 poems of 14 lines of interwoven rhyme, first published in 1609, that form a loose sequence. Shakespeare's sonnets are at once the apex of the form, representing the heights of what it can achieve, and also an afterword to a poetic tradition that had dominated literary fashion some twenty years earlier; the 1590s saw sonnet sequences by Philip Sidney, Edmund Spenser, Richard Barnfield, Samuel Daniel and others, and it may have been during this period that Shakespeare first worked on his own poems. An element of belatedness is central to our understanding of the sonnets, and to this book; our poets, like Shakespeare himself, are returning to a form that is itself propelled by the logic of return, as its rhyme sounds constantly bring the reader back to preceding lines, making the past vividly present in the current moment.

One of the preoccupations of Shakespeare's series is with how the poet and his lovers will be remembered after they are gone. As such, the sonnets make a particularly fitting place at which to pause and commemorate Shakespeare himself. The themes of loss, grief, the passing of time, mortality, and posthumous remembrance that pervade the sequence have proved enduring; our own poets frequently take them up here, and, like Shakespeare, explore such terrain as a way of thinking about what poetry itself can do. When Shakespeare imagines his own poems as 'the living record of *your* memory', he speaks of each reader's ability to bring life to his verse, as well as his verse's ability to memorialize the beloved. There is a knowing bravado there too, and these new poems respond to the cynical competitiveness of the sonnet, as well as its capacity for more reverent celebration.

A concern with inheritance – the transmission of ideas, values, and even words, from one generation to another – often guides the writers assembled here, who look to the past and its literary riches as well as to the future and their own legacies. This past is at once a source of inspiration and a shadow any writer must step out of; Shakespeare felt this acutely, and now he himself casts perhaps the longest shadow of all. The desire to emulate and surpass the writers of the past drove Shakespeare to new literary heights, while rivalry with his contemporaries prompted some of the most astonishing theatrical and poetic experiments ever known.

This potent combination of past tradition and individual innovation makes Shakespeare's voice unique. His metaphors, in particular, deserve comment for their power, aptness and sheer unexpected beauty. Shakespeare remakes the language afresh, and our poets in turn rework the imaginative landscape of poetry here. Sleep is figured as the sea, ebbing and flowing to its own rhythms. A fragile flower or plant comes to hold the weight of the universe. A storm summons up all the forces of nature and human invention. The sonnet form requires that each poem is often built around one such image – or conceit – exploring a metaphor by turning it inside out. The 'volta', or turn, that comes in the latter lines of each sonnet gives this particular force, allowing a poet to radically rethink his or her own ideas within the security of a tightly constrained form. Our contributors have seized this imperative and often borrow the logic of the Shakespearean sonnet even where they do not choose write in this form themselves. The skeleton of such poems, which are usually structured in two units of eight and then six lines, but which retain a sense of quatrains and a couplet, prompts numerological play and allows a writer to create a counterpoint between the movement of a poem and the differing rhythms of the ideas it contains. Again, Shakespeare does this to a super-lative degree, and our poets have internalized this aspect of his writing, giving it new life in their own verse. The sonnet is at once the most compressed of literary forms, and also one of the most expansive. Like Shakespeare, it contains multitudes. We believe the poems in this collection do the same.

Hannah Crawforth and Elizabeth Scott-Baumann

King's College London

Acknowledgements

Foremost thanks are due to the thirty poets who wrote for this collection. The editors would like to thank Margaret Bartley and Emily Hockley at Bloomsbury Arden Shakespeare; Cortina Butler and the British Council; Eleanor Crawforth; Maggie Fergusson and the Royal Society of Literature; Hadrian, Lucian and Rufus Green; David Harsent; Andrew Motion and the Poetry Archive; Gordon McMullan, Clare Whitehead, the English Department, the London Shakespeare Centre, the Arts and Humanities Research Institute and the Faculty of Arts and Humanities at King's College London; Fiona Sampson; Colin Thubron; Benjie and Edward Way.

Bloomsbury Arden Shakespeare provided the text of *Shakespeare's Sonnets* edited by Katherine Duncan-Jones.

What poverty my Muse brings forth
(A Cento)

Roger McGough

O from what power hast thou this powerful might
O how thy worth with manners may I sing
O how I faint when I of you do write
Farewell, thou art too dear for my possessing.
If thou survive my well-contented day
Who is it that says most? Which can say more?
How heavy do I journey on the way
Like as the waves make towards the pebbled shore.
Those lines that I before have writ do lie
Weary with toil, I haste me to my bed.
Tired with all these for restful death I cry
No longer mourn for me when I am dead.
   Poor soul, the centre of my sinful earth
   Alack, what poverty my Muse brings forth.

1

From fairest creatures we desire increase,
That thereby beauty's rose might never die,
But as the riper should by time decease
His tender heir might bear his memory:
But thou, contracted to thine own bright eyes,
Feed'st thy light's flame with self-substantial fuel,
Making a famine where abundance lies,
Thyself thy foe, to thy sweet self too cruel.
Thou that art now the world's fresh ornament,
And only herald to the gaudy spring,
Within thine own bud buriest thy content,
And, tender churl, mak'st waste in niggarding.
    Pity the world, or else this glutton be,
    To eat the world's due, by the grave and thee.

Senex on Market Street

Douglas Dunn

'Thou that art now the world's fresh ornament'

Posh totty totters past on serious heels.
In handsomeness, with confidence, they walk
Towards exams, and don't know how it feels
To hear the fateful tick-tock of the clock.
Young women, and young men, I, too, was young –
Believe that if you can! – but years go by
Until, one day, you find your songs are sung;
Ambitionless, your sap and tears run dry.
There's something I must tell – need you know this? –
I loved a woman who dressed as well as you;
But I can't give the past false emphasis,
For even old love is for ever new.
    When she walked out she dulcified the air;
    And so do you. To say so's only fair.

11

As fast as thou shalt wane, so fast thou grow'st
In one of thine, from that which thou departest;
And that fresh blood which youngly thou bestow'st
Thou mayst call thine, when thou from youth
            convertest;
Herein lives wisdom, beauty and increase;
Without this, folly, age and cold decay.
If all were minded so, the times should cease,
And threescore year would make the world away:
Let those whom nature hath not made for store,
Harsh, featureless and rude, barrenly perish;
Look whom she best endowed, she gave the more,
Which bounteous gift thou shouldst in bounty cherish:
  She carved thee for her seal, and meant thereby
  Thou shouldst print more, not let that copy die.

Thirty-Five

Jackie Kay

As quick as you fell ill, quickly you recover;
A quip returned, a memory uncovered.
Saline drip, subcut, a new route discovered.
You slip into the railed bed, slide under covers.
Outside Glasgow Royal – snow – a thin sheet.
Inside your wit, wisdom makes my heart swell –
Bigger than your water-retaining feet.
Without this love, nothing could ever be well.
A gift the heart wrapped early in this life.
The more you give the more you have to cherish.
If I could offer you my veins, I'd gladly use a knife.
At times it seems if you go, I too will perish.

    A mould broke made a new mother of you.
    Blood, water, sealed with a kiss: all true.

12

When I do count the clock that tells the time,
And see the brave day sunk in hideous night;
When I behold the violet past prime,
And sable curls all silvered o'er with white:
When lofty trees I see barren of leaves,
Which erst from heat did canopy the herd,
And summer's green all girded up in sheaves
Borne on the bier with white and bristly beard:
Then of thy beauty do I question make,
That thou among the wastes of time must go,
Since sweets and beauties do themselves forsake,
And die as fast as they see others grow,

    And nothing 'gainst time's scythe can make defence
    Save breed to brave him, when he takes thee hence.

Rhapsodies

Andrew Motion

12: When I do count the clock that tells the time

The clocks change, and there's suddenly the shock
of walking home in darkness, seeing lights
inside the windows, thinking Who lives there?
Whose books are those? Whose ornaments? Who chose
that purple orchid flowering on that shelf?
And then remembering or better still
accepting: me, I live there, me with you –
and yes of course my key fits in the lock.
At which another suddenly: the sound
of you already back and practising.
I recognise it. Brahms; Two Rhapsodies;
the notes that stayed invisible all day
sweep in like birds through newly-blackened air
and land in time to sing before they sleep.

30: When to the sessions of sweet silent thought

We found each other late, by winding roads,
and for my own part: when I saw you clear
I saw you through the glass of my mistakes
which I can only think weren't dear time's waste
if I believe they taught me how to live.
Live better, that's to say, although to fail
less hurtfully and with more care might be
a straighter way of saying what I feel.
Forgive me, then, for what you do not know.
Forgive me for the vanities that now
allow me to suggest they're finished; gone.
They're not, of course – all losses are restored –
but loving you as who I was made new,
at least the chance exists they might be less.

74: But be contented when that fell arrest

I can't not think, although I wish I could,
of life alone for one of us at last:
daybreak and no dreams to tell and hear;
the silent meals with food that can't be faced;
your clothes, or mine, still huddled in their rows
until such time as we dare pass them on;
and always, with the guilt built into grief,
the sense of life now lost not lived enough.
And yet (our instinct always wants 'and yet')
the earth can have but earth, which is his due,
while something else, which neither of us likes
to give a name, will stay for who remains.
Already, sometimes, when an old day ends,
I think the next might bring it round again.

146: Poor soul, the centre of my sinful earth

I finish where I started: in the world
of hard occasions. Clocks are forward now
and though we lose an hour it seems much more,
the benefit of evenings in the light
offset by knowing time itself is short.
How many springs, when this spring finishes?
How many summer days before they turn
to old December's bareness everywhere?
And consolation? If that comes at all
it comes from looking back on finished time
as much as making sure we spend each now
and now and now and now and now, until
we learn to feed on death, that feeds on us
although we know full well how that must end.

15

When I consider everything that grows
Holds in perfection but a little moment;
That this huge stage presenteth naught but shows
Whereon the stars in secret influence comment;
When I perceive that men as plants increase,
Cheered and checked even by the self-same sky,
Vaunt in their youthful sap, at height decrease,
And wear their brave state out of memory:
Then the conceit of this inconstant stay
Sets you, most rich in youth, before my sight,
Where wasteful time debateth with decay
To change your day of youth to sullied night:
    And all in war with time for love of you
    As he takes from you, I engraft you new.

Sonnet 15: A Graft

Paul Muldoon

The hedge between us and Grew's orchard grows
no less tenaciously than at the moment
its quickset cuttings took, though now it shows
white- and black-thorn interspersed with a comment
from a briar rose. Sometimes an increase
in the percentage of rose hips in the sky
has seen a corresponding decrease
in haws and sloes. What burgeons in the memory
is how a stroke of your penknife could stay
us against the future … What's in plain sight
quite often stems from darkness and decay –
day's being grafted to the stock of night
    a thought compounded by the cow dung you
    had plastered there till old wood wrote the new.

18

Shall I compare thee to a summer's day?
Thou art more lovely and more temperate:
Rough winds do shake the darling buds of May,
And summer's lease hath all too short a date:
Sometime too hot the eye of heaven shines,
And often is his gold complexion dimmed;
And every fair from fair sometime declines,
By chance, or nature's changing course, untrimmed:
But thy eternal summer shall not fade,
Nor lose possession of that fair thou ow'st,
Nor shall death brag thou wander'st in his shade
When in eternal lines to time thou grow'st:
    So long as men can breathe or eyes can see,
    So long lives this, and this gives life to thee.

Dream

P. J. Kavanagh

Exaggeration is the role of art!
Because we are tiny creations – yet not so.
On dreams can fall a grandeur and the heart
Speak languages we waking do not know:
Your face, behind a window, its sash-cord stuck;
You struggle to open it; railings are too tall
For me to climb and help. But, trusting luck,
Soon we are crossing on foot a Javanese mall
In murderous traffic. Apart, not hand in hand,
You first, (and this seemed right); we keep our angle,
Oblique, unvaried. Today we are still bound
Not by a chain or a rope, by a radio-signal
   Of exaggeration, never untuned, a wireless
   Connection, with its own reach and sound – and tireless.

20

A woman's face with nature's own hand painted
Hast thou, the master mistress of my passion;
A woman's gentle heart, but not acquainted
With shifting change, as is false women's fashion;
An eye more bright than theirs, less false in rolling,
Gilding the object whereupon it gazeth;
A man in hue, all hues in his controlling,
Which steals men's eyes and women's souls amazeth;
And for a woman wert thou first created,
Till nature as she wrought thee fell a-doting,
And by addition me of thee defeated,
By adding one thing to my purpose nothing:
    But since she pricked thee out for women's pleasure,
    Mine be thy love, and thy love's use their treasure.

Di-Di-Dah-Dah-Di-Dit

Simon Armitage

di-di-di-dit   dit   di-dah-di-dit   dah-dah-dah
di-di-di-dah   dit
di-di-dit   di-di-di-dit   di-dit   dah-dah
di-di-di-dit

dit   di-dah-di-dit   dah-dah-dah
di-di-di-dah   dit   di-di-dit   di-di-di-dit
di-dit   dah-dah   dah-dit   dah-dah-dah   dah
di-di-di-dit   dit   di-dah-di-dit

dah-dah-dah   di-di-di-dah
dit   di-di-dit   di-di-di-dit   di-dit
dah-dah   di-di-di-dit   dit   di-dah-di-dit   dah-dah-dah
di-di-di-dah   dit   di-di-dit

di-di-di-dit   di-dit   dah-dah
dah-dit   dah-dah-dah   dah

22

My glass shall not persuade me I am old
So long as youth and thou are of one date;
But when in thee time's furrows I behold,
Then look I death my days should expiate:
For all that beauty that doth cover thee
Is but the seemly raiment of my heart,
Which in thy breast doth live, as thine in me;
How can I then be elder than thou art?
O therefore love be of thyself so wary
As I not for myself, but for thee will,
Bearing thy heart, which I will keep so chary
As tender nurse her babe from faring ill:
    Presume not on thy heart when mine is slain;
    Thou gav'st me thine not to give back again.

Sonnet

Wendy Cope

My glass can't quite persuade me I am old –
In that respect my ageing eyes are kind –
But when I see a photograph, I'm told
The dismal truth: I've left my youth behind.
And when I try to get up from a chair
My knees remind me they are past their best.
The burden they have carried everywhere
Is heavier now. No wonder they protest.
Arthritic fingers, problematic neck,
Sometimes causing mild to moderate pain,
Could well persuade me I'm an ancient wreck
But here's what helps me to feel young again:
    My love, who fell for me so long ago,
    Still loves me just as much, and tells me so.

33

Full many a glorious morning have I seen
Flatter the mountain tops with sovereign eye,
Kissing with golden face the meadows green,
Gilding pale streams with heavenly alchemy;
Anon permit the basest clouds to ride
With ugly rack on his celestial face,
And from the forlorn world his visage hide,
Stealing unseen to west with this disgrace:
Even so my sun one early morn did shine
With all triumphant splendour on my brow;
But out alack, he was but one hour mine,
The region cloud hath masked him from me now.
    Yet him for this, my love no whit disdaineth:
    Suns of the world may stain, when heaven's sun
        staineth.

Hearing Voices

Mimi Khalvati

'Yes, you were, you were', I laughed, 'golden children!'
Through all those years of hubris, me taking pride,
As though it were my doing, in that golden,
Blameless childhood, you with no cause to hide
Anything more than boyhood's guilty pleasures.
But how you hid when the sky split, the voices came,
Each with a face you drew, wild familiars,
Grotesques that only talking to could tame.
Then on their heels crept silences: your childhood,
Mother, father, sister, all held at bay,
All suspect. Illness might be in the blood,
Even how we laugh in our DNA.
    Yet how we laughed, there in the sun that spread
    Through leaves and seemed to gild what my son said!

35

No more be grieved at that which thou hast done;
Roses have thorns, and silver fountains mud;
Clouds and eclipses stain both moon and sun,
And loathsome canker lives in sweetest bud.
All men make faults, and even I, in this,
Authorizing thy trespass with compare,
Myself corrupting, salving thy amiss,
Excusing these sins more than these sins are:
For to thy sensual fault I bring in sense;
Thy adverse party is thy advocate,
And 'gainst myself a lawful plea commence:
Such civil war is in my love and hate
    That I an accessory needs must be
    To that sweet thief which sourly robs from me.

Peacemaker

Michael Symmons Roberts

To put this civil war to bed at last,
I step offstage, watch sex scenes from the wings,
our lives played out by better-looking cast,
forbidden lovers pocketing their rings.

It's safe out here, beyond the sonnet's frame,
(though I can mouth the words before they're said)
my love as metadrama: burlesque games,
a tragedy where no-one winds up dead.

But as my hapless actor shouts the odds,
hands shaking as they hold your sobbing face,
it sounds like melodrama, from the gods –
who cares who is betrayed and who betrays?

I lay the ceasefire treaties out to sign:
a caveat, a sub-clause, more delays.
Meanwhile, on stage, he busks a fifteenth line.

36

Let me confess that we two must be twain,
Although our undivided loves are one;
So shall those blots that do with me remain,
Without thy help, by me be borne alone.
In our two loves there is but one respect,
Though in our lives a separable spite;
Which, though it alter not love's sole effect,
Yet doth it steal sweet hours from love's delight.
I may not evermore acknowledge thee,
Lest my bewailed guilt should do thee shame,
Nor thou with public kindness honour me,
Unless thou take that honour from thy name:
    But do not so; I love thee in such sort,
    As thou being mine, mine is thy good report.

Two

Don Paterson

These two, if two, can only half-exist,
their being so lost, so inwardly inclined
that were somehow the universal mind
to make its inventory, they would be missed,
their bodies having slipped between the hours
and dropped down to this silent underland,
the white torque of their sheet still in her hand
like the means of their escape. From the light purse
of their mouths, they pass their only coin
endlessly, so none may buy or sell.
Each has drawn so long and drank so deep
from the other's throat or root, they cannot tell
tongue from tail or end from origin.
Sleep will halve them so they will not sleep.

38

How can my Muse want subject to invent
While thou dost breathe, that pour'st into my verse
Thine own sweet argument, too excellent
For every vulgar paper to rehearse?
O give thyself the thanks, if aught in me
Worthy perusal stand against thy sight:
For who's so dumb, that cannot write to thee,
When thou thyself dost give invention light?
Be thou the tenth Muse, ten times more in worth
Than those old nine which rhymers invocate;
And he that calls on thee, let him bring forth
Eternal numbers to outlive long date.
    If my slight Muse do please these curious days,
    The pain be mine, but thine shall be the praise.

After Sonnet 38

Nick Laird

Love, if I call them in from the darkness,
the sonneteers, our fabulous liars,
and get them to sit at these rows of desks,
distribute goose quills, rolls of papyrus
or vellum sheets, or slates, or MacBook Airs,
disable the wifi and monitor
lighting, the background sounds and temperatures,
divert the Polish cleaner and offer
bottomless coffee or a few wee nips,
then set each brother at the other's throat
with talk of posterity, the odd gift
of hard cash, and stand at the back to wait –
for as long as they want – for years and years –
they could not start to get down half your ways.

43

When most I wink, then do mine eyes best see;
For all the day they view things unrespected,
But when I sleep, in dreams they look on thee,
And darkly bright, are bright in dark directed.
Then thou whose shadow shadows doth make bright,
How would thy shadow's form form happy show
To the clear day with thy much clearer light,
When to unseeing eyes thy shade shines so?
How would (I say) mine eyes be blessed made
By looking on thee in the living day,
When in dead night thy fair imperfect shade
Through heavy sleep on sightless eyes doth stay?
    All days are nights to see till I see thee,
    And nights bright days when dreams do show
        thee me.

The Trick

Imtiaz Dharker

In a wasted time, it's only when I sleep
that all my senses come awake. In the wake
of you, let day not break. Let me keep
the scent, the weight, the bright of you, take
the countless hours and count them all night through
till that time comes when you come to the door
of dreams, carrying oranges that cast a glow
up into your face. Greedy for more
than the gift of seeing you, I lean in to taste
the colour, kiss it off your offered mouth.
For this, for this, I fall asleep in haste,
willing to fall for the trick that tells the truth
    that even your shade makes darkest absence bright,
    that shadows live wherever there is light.

49

Against that time, if ever that time come,
When I shall see thee frown on my defects;
Whenas thy love hath cast his utmost sum,
Called to that audit by advised respects;
Against that time when thou shalt strangely pass,
And scarcely greet me with that sun, thine eye;
When love, converted from the thing it was,
Shall reasons find of settled gravity;
Against that time do I ensconce me here,
Within the knowledge of mine own desert,
And this my hand against myself uprear,
To guard the lawful reasons on thy part:

    To leave poor me, thou hast the strength of laws,
    Since why to love, I can allege no cause.

At the Hallé

Bernard O'Donoghue

He sat by her side, near the front, sideways on
to the cellos and the second violins
under the gold blazon of the brass section.
He feared she'd see if he risked a sideways glance,
looking for some imperfection that would mean
he was not so totally outclassed:
her nose slightly too big; the small blemish
on her left cheek (the right as you looked at it)
which you could only see when you enlarged
her image on the screen of the computer.
Around her eyes, he knew, were thin, tired lines,
and under them were deeper lines – 'bags' even –
under the right eye in particular.

In due course a time would surely come
when he would find nothing much endearing
in her blemishes and would wonder
if he might have done better for himself.

But he was very far from that point yet
as he faced the music, taking comfort in
his full appreciation of the harmonies.

55

Not marble, nor the gilded monuments
Of princes, shall outlive this powerful rhyme;
But you shall shine more bright in these contents
Than unswept stone, besmeared with sluttish time.
When wasteful war shall statues overturn
And broils root out the work of masonry,
Nor Mars his sword, nor war's quick fire, shall burn
The living record of your memory:
'Gainst death, and all oblivious enmity,
Shall you pace forth; your praise shall still find room
Even in the eyes of all posterity
That wear this world out to the ending doom.
   So till the judgement that yourself arise,
   You live in this, and dwell in lovers' eyes.

The Sonnets

Michael Longley

for Vanessa Davis

The soldier-poet packed into his kitbag
His spine-protector, socks, soap, latherbrush
(Though he was not then a regular shaver)
Water-bottle, field-dressing, gas-mask, a tin
Of cigarettes (a gift from Princess Mary,
The girl next door at Buckingham Palace),
Housewife, bootlaces, pull-through, paybook
And the sonnets of William Shakespeare.

He brushed off the mud at Passchendaele and,
Before going over the top, tucked away
In his breast pocket the leather-bound book,
Which stopped a bullet just short of his heart
And shredded the life-saving poetry. He
Inhaled one of Princess Mary's Woodbines.

60

Like as the waves make towards the pebbled shore,
So do our minutes hasten to their end,
Each changing place with that which goes before,
In sequent toil all forwards do contend.
Nativity, once in the main of light,
Crawls to maturity; wherewith being crowned
Crooked eclipses 'gainst his glory fight,
And time, that gave, doth now his gift confound.
Time doth transfix the flourish set on youth,
And delves the parallels in beauty's brow;
Feeds on the rarities of nature's truth,
And nothing stands but for his scythe to mow.
   And yet to times in hope my verse shall stand,
   Praising thy worth, despite his cruel hand.

Time's Fool

Kevin Crossley-Holland

Ocean's always more than we can make of it,
a better metaphor than any for two-handed time.

Swashbuckle, yes, and silver spears shaking,
that's how it is at the top of the tide,

but each wave breaking grows reluctant
to sort shingle, dissolve casts, even to adjust

that scribble of froth and stringy weed,
seacoal, mermaids' purses, bottles, brattlings.

Tide on the drag (after the equipoise)
lays bare our whole expanse of days

– momentary migrants reflected in water,
skimming over the foreshore, its shallows

and snags, hidden clear-eyed pools –
and then it summons from the deep

raven Thought, cormorant Memory.
Before tide's down and out, sandflats and slakes

become teeming wordbeds, salty and lucent,
where it's time always to address time.

Your Life as a Wave

Ruth Padel

'...*like travellers ahead of me on the journey, I'd like to ask them,
Is the way smooth and easy, or rugged and difficult?*'

Plato, *Republic*, Book 1

Born in the main of light, lily-fire on the horizon,
you find little specks of you, sympathy, projection,
jealousy and love, fly out and lodge in other people.
You become a spirit of the water
governed by the moon, luminous as the veil
of the Medusa. You dance in spray like pear blossom –
a childhood free as the soprano
of Victoria de los Angeles in *Songs of the Auvergne*.
But then storms blow you haywire. Time,
which used to be your friend, turns traitor.
What with the replaced hip, lost words
and fading memories, Time speeds up to a roar
of ocean currents and you lose your self
in frazzles of sliding foam on the pebbled shore.

That's one version. But what about free will,
the self re-cycled, dreams of other worlds
and journeys to enlightenment?
Let's reverse the metaphor, say you were born
here where the tide comes in, with seeds

of what you may become concealed in bladder-wrack
like the carbon star in a trapiche emerald.
The ripple-lace of surf: *that's* where the wave begins.
Fonteyne not as dying swan but bright Undine.
Yes, say we move towards uncharted beauty. Age
means no more living on a knife-edge,
drawing up the dark like blood in a syringe,
but pure delight in slatted shadows on the wall,
a sunlit garden, sudden flight of goldfinches.
You gaze out at the night, and see a square of yellow
where there was, or used to be, no house. Want to re-find
who you were? You never can. There's only *on*,
away from the pebbled shore to the main of light.

65

Since brass, nor stone, nor earth, nor boundless sea,
But sad mortality o'er-sways their power,
How with this rage shall beauty hold a plea,
Whose action is no stronger than a flower?
O how shall summer's honey breath hold out
Against the wrackful siege of batt'ring days
When rocks impregnable are not so stout,
Nor gates of steel so strong, but time decays?
O fearful meditation! Where, alack,
Shall time's best jewel from time's chest lie hid?
Or what strong hand can hold his swift foot back,
Or who his spoil o'er beauty can forbid?
   O none, unless this miracle have might:
   That in black ink my love may still shine bright.

Storm, Nissaki

Robin Robertson

The sky claps once, then throws itself open; the room
flares wide and white

and jolts sideways, jumping the rails.
Sheet lightning – lighting the night to *before*

and *after*: after-images of black and white.
At each flash the room leaps, across itself

to the other side, from a black box to a box of light. The sky
opens its hands and claps them shut; thunder stoops

to shiver the house's great stone bell. Another strike
takes a snapshot of me, there on the jetty; an epileptic

kick of lightning and I'm scribbled out clear –
this pale, forked nib of a life.

The room sits up suddenly, bright as a photo-booth,
then turns on its side like the sea.

Two Sonnets

Alan Brownjohn

(1) A Winter Elegy
i.m. Erzsébet Ádám, Teatrul National

A valley outside town. Winter. Earth. Stone.
Today Time's judgement holds, that you lie here
In a dark portion of his chest which none
Save he will guard; and let no light shine near,
Unless some hand contrive to oversway
His power with such strong actions as I think
Might flower in summer, on a lovelier day,
In written lines, in bright, enduring ink.
Then would you live, and all your fairest parts
Be so remembered beyond boundless seas
For the rarest jewels, inside all loving hearts
Hidden away from Time's foul jealousies.
    Let these words serve as Prologue to an act
    Cruel Time shall envy when it is a fact.

(2) A Call

'That was her ringing. Saying we should come
At half-past twelve for coffee and sandwiches.
Then there's to be a short symposium
With actors, directors and celebrities
It would help you to meet. And they'd be sure
To enjoy meeting you, seeing they rarely get
The chance to talk with someone from somewhere
The theatre's so incredible …' – And yet
What I most remember is you had to have
A picture with her! She said 'Yes', on one condition
– That any photograph she agreed to give
Should only ever be used with her permission.

   – You observed that. It was only brought out today,
   One in your last publicity display.

71

No longer mourn for me when I am dead
Than you shall hear the surly sullen bell
Give warning to the world that I am fled
From this vile world, with vilest worms to dwell:
Nay, if you read this line, remember not
The hand that writ it, for I love you so
That I in your sweet thoughts would be forgot,
If thinking on me then should make you woe.
O if (I say) you look upon this verse,
When I, perhaps, compounded am with clay,
Do not so much as my poor name rehearse,
But let your love even with my life decay;
    Lest the wise world should look into your moan,
    And mock you with me after I am gone.

Still Life

John Burnside

You know where this work begins: a brace of quail
or woodcock; half a dozen

oysters, shucked, and spending in a slur
of milt and light; a bowl from Jingdezhen,

brought in, they say, as ballast for the tea,
(that blue and white the Chinese did not favour,

preferring single tones, say *lang yao hong,*
or *qingbai*, threads

of craquelure or pooling in the glaze
instead of narrative), the emblematic

lotus bloom or Willow Pattern scene
half-hidden by a heap of blemished grapes

and vineleaf, peaches, lemons with their rinds
half-peeled. It has nothing to do

with shellfish, nothing to do
with cherries, or the trade in porcelain,

but speaks of how the worm
is present, always: moments as they happen

perishable, married love and selfhood
perishable by their very

nature; yet, by nature, given back
in season, sieved

through clay and rain and fruit-falls for the meagre
gold of summer's end, the kitchen

silent, when you bring the apples in
and wrap them, individually, in sheets

of newsprint, humming torch songs to yourself
till dusk, beyond the point where I am gone.

73

That time of year thou mayst in me behold,
When yellow leaves, or none, or few do hang
Upon those boughs which shake against the cold,
Bare ruined choirs where late the sweet birds sang;
In me thou seest the twilight of such day
As after sunset fadeth in the west,
Which by and by black night doth take away,
Death's second self that seals up all in rest;
In me thou seest the glowing of such fire
That on the ashes of his youth doth lie,
As the deathbed, whereon it must expire,
Consumed with that which it was nourished by;
   This thou perceiv'st, which makes thy love more
      strong,
   To love that well, which thou must leave ere long.

73 Shakespeare Close

David Harsent

She went straight to his house and somehow let herself in.
Blue was a colour he favoured, that much was plain.
The shirts in his closet were blue and blue again.
She put one on. She wanted to drown in blue.
She wanted to talk to someone, but didn't know who.
She wanted the weather to turn. She wanted rain.

Imagine music in air, a creeping stain
much like a bruise that darkened as it grew;
imagine her fixed in the moment, imagine pain
as one with the music, as blue beneath the skin.
Suddenly nothing was safe and nothing true,
nothing that anger could govern or love explain,
though her breathless stillness brought on the rain: a clue
to what she could never avoid and never undo.

2014/2015

Jo Shapcott

We name our years in numbers and behold, I said,
this new one hangs ahead, plump and divisible.
I poked my cold head round the corner of December,
whose bare evenings sang to me of the future,
until I could see all 365 days laid out from east
to west. A few things stick with me:
a sea view, night-time, lights across the by and by,
wet, black shapes, perhaps the heads of seals;
the Northern Line, glowing with afterworkers –
and someone humming, unless the future is a lie;
a laptop screen: keystrokes and the words expire,
metadata, prism, nourished, homeland, boundless
informant. My beloveds, I will see all this
and I will leave it, in one order or another, to you.

80

O how I faint when I of you do write,
Knowing a better spirit doth use your name,
And in the praise thereof spends all his might,
To make me tongue-tied speaking of your fame.
But since your worth, wide as the ocean is,
The humble as the proudest sail doth bear,
My saucy bark, inferior far to his,
On your broad main doth wilfully appear.
Your shallowest help will hold me up afloat,
Whilst he upon your soundless deep doth ride;
Or, being wracked, I am a worthless boat,
He of tall building, and of goodly pride.
    Then if he thrive, and I be cast away,
    The worst was this: my love was my decay.

Salvage

Alan Jenkins

You had read of his disturbing exploits
Before we'd even met – compared to him
I was a schoolboy playing deck-quoits,

One eye on you slumped in your lounger,
The thin bikini-thing stretched across your quim.
He was a lord of language, I a saloon-bar scrounger.

I dreamt of sailing *Spray* – grandfather Herrick's
Little sloop – from its berth in an old black-and-white
Past the dockside forest of cranes and derricks

And the rusted cliff-face of a super-tanker
To a secluded cove. He rules the bight
Where his Clipper-class yacht rides at anchor.

His triumphs enlarge you, I see that, and your largesse
Puts wind in his sails. If one day, on a whim
You had a go with me, you'd be a mere bargess

To my bargee – and who would want that, really?
I salvage what I can from knowing that some doors
Are open to me on your say-so merely.

On top of all this, the proud pennants, the prizes,
The fame he owes to you! (As you owe yours,
Admittedly, to him.) No-one capsizes

When there is so much that's keeping them
Afloat, when they can boast such perfect trim.
While the sea-floors, and the job of sweeping them,

Are my concern. And I can't help but wonder –
Though I know you both hold that it's sink or swim –
Why it should be me who's going under.

94

They that have power to hurt, and will do none,
That do not do the thing they most do show,
Who, moving others, are themselves as stone,
Unmoved, cold, and to temptation slow:
They rightly do inherit heaven's graces,
And husband nature's riches from expense;
They are the lords and owners of their faces,
Others, but stewards of their excellence.
The summer's flower is to the summer sweet,
Though to itself it only live and die,
But if that flower with base infection meet,
The basest weed outbraves his dignity:
    For sweetest things turn sourest by their deeds;
    Lilies that fester smell far worse than weeds.

Three Views of a Secret

Sean O'Brien

i

Is it that all you are is beautiful,
The world your elegant sufficiency,
A balcony on which you may arrive
Spontaneously once more to blind us all
With your neglectful gaze – *choose me, choose me* –
Itself an end, which means we are alive
To suffer in the service of the will
You do not choose to exercise? Do tell.
The stars' exertions staring down the dark
Are all extinguished by comparison
With your implacable indifference.
Show us again, *show me*, the cruel sense
You make, although I know there can be none,
Then when I sicken, kill me with a look.

ii

The mirror is expecting you. You're late.
Should silver blacken, flesh give up its bone,
Time will attend you still, and after that
More time, when all your suitors go to dust.
It is a law and strikes down both the just
And the unjust, pronouncing them the same
Poor tenants of your comfortless estate.
Oh all the rest are gone like a rehearsal.
The mirror waits for you to come to pass.
To think they said you could not have it all:
As you have learned from gazing in the glass,
The mirror waits. It waits for you alone.
The only answer to this world is one.

iii

When you consume yourself away, the room
Grows sober in the aftermath. The light
Falls plainly on the bare bed and the chair.
Now it might seem that you were never there.
Your exit, like your law, is absolute,
Your legacy intolerable calm,
The blaze of noon identical with night
And ecstasy the servant of despair.
You will not serve the downcast god of love:
That great refusal is a gift I crave.
Yours is the power to steal the world away
And to possess what might have been its soul
In patience, as one might possess a grave
Before the spade has even pierced the soil.

99

The forward violet thus did I chide:
'Sweet thief, whence didst thou steal thy sweet that
        smells,
If not from my love's breath? The purple pride
Which on thy soft cheek for complexion dwells
In my love's veins thou hast too grossly dyed.'
The lily I condemned for thy hand,
And buds of marjoram had stol'n thy hair;
The roses fearfully on thorns did stand,
One blushing shame, another white despair;
A third, nor red, nor white, had stol'n of both,
And to his robb'ry had annexed thy breath;
But for his theft, in pride of all his growth,
A vengeful canker ate him up to death.
    More flowers I noted, yet I none could see,
    But sweet, or colour, it had stol'n from thee.

Gentian Violet

Paul Farley

Finding a roadside gentian activates
a sunset clause in the laws of common sense:
as I'm about to nick it from this verge
the flower sends a little shock to my hand.
The rainbow runs to earth: beyond here
it's all geophysics, worms, Pluto's blue torch
in the MRI, where flowers are the wounds
they once were gathered to heal, it's a certain stain
in a sweetheart deal with bees, cut flower scents
during the night feed on a ward, it's the vein
that rises for a moment in your breast.
Now the flower blooms harder, the way a fire
in a city, seen from air support, shorts out
a block or two of power around itself
and cultivates more dark to flare against.

116

Let me not to the marriage of true minds
Admit impediments; love is not love
Which alters when it alteration finds,
Or bends with the remover to remove.
O no, it is an ever-fixed mark,
That looks on tempests and is never shaken;
It is the star to every wand'ring bark,
Whose worth's unknown, although his height be taken.
Love's not Time's fool, though rosy lips and cheeks
Within his bending sickle's compass come;
Love alters not with his brief hours and weeks,
But bears it out even to the edge of doom.
   If this be error and upon me proved,
   I never writ, nor no man ever loved.

Magnetism

Gillian Clarke

Pull between earth and moon, or chemistry,
carries the swallow home from Africa
to perch again on his remembered tree,
the weeping birch by the pond. A star
will guide his mate home in a week, perhaps,
to the old nest in the barn, remade, mould
of spittle and pond-sludge snug in its cusp
as the new year in the mud-cup of the old.
Loss broke the swan on the river when winter
stole his mate when he wasn't looking. Believing,
he waited, rebuilt the nest, all summer
holding their stretch of river, raging, grieving.

So would I wait for you, were we put apart.
Mind, magnetism, hunger of the heart.

CXVI

Carol Ann Duffy

Our two heads on one pillow; I awake
to hear impediments scratch in the room
like rats. I let you sleep, dream on. Your face
is summer, cloudless, innocent; it blooms.
My kiss, a dying bee grazing a rose.

Something is wrong. Or let a poem prove
the star we followed more than failing light
from time long gone. Love is not love.
Your heart on mine, I feel, a marriage rite –
but on the floor there lie no wedding clothes.

Don't stir. The curtains won't allow the sun.
Our minds are distant; sullen earth, cold moon.
Out of the corner of my eye, I see them flit,
dark shadows, verminous. Let me admit…

Betrayal

Elaine Feinstein

Get over it, get a life, my friends implore me,
    sure that revival lies in moving on.
Yet some bond holds me like a tie of blood,
    as inescapable as the loyalty
formed in my father-adoring childhood.
    I can go anywhere now you are gone

but everywhere else is where I feel alone.
    Is that need for you – *love* ?
There are harsher words. And cowardice is one,
    another, pride – I never could get rid of
my spoilt child's sullen grip on a possession –
    I call it desperation

not to give up what once held us together:
    our bodies' casual tenderness –
our sleep's embrace become a natural tether.
    Defeating loneliness,
we both found home in a shared family nest
    and our licensed disorder.

Must I abandon that long happiness?
      Visits from old lovers easily
stir sexual memories but I confess
      none of them now arouse me:
at best, they feel somehow irrelevant.
      I cannot fake excitement,

I'll wait – though the rejected rarely win.
      Let's have no reassurance:
If you come back, of course I'll let you in –
      but it will take endurance.
We are one flesh. Your guilt will punish me.
      We shall both bear the pain of treachery.

143

Lo, as a careful housewife runs to catch
One of her feathered creatures broke away,
Sets down her babe, and makes all swift dispatch
In pursuit of the thing she would have stay;
Whilst her neglected child holds her in chase,
Cries to catch her whose busy care is bent
To follow that which flies before her face,
Not prizing her poor infant's discontent:
So run'st thou after that which flies from thee,
Whilst I, thy babe, chase thee afar behind.
But if thou catch thy hope, turn back to me,
And play the mother's part, kiss me, be kind:
　　So will I pray that thou mayst have thy Will,
　　If thou turn back and my loud crying still.

Drowned Man

Fiona Sampson

Holds him in chase

Look how they sleep first he turns
away and then she turns
after him or now she turns
her back and he follows

rolled by an old imperative
deeper than sleep
he rolls over like a wave
that turns itself over

sleepily with the sea's deep
breathing with its rhythm
pulsing far out from land pulsing far
down in the dark

where creatures not yet formed are forming
where like half-made beasts
his dreams swim among hers where
she hears his breathing far

above her nearer to the light
nearer to the white-topped
waves the white-peaked sheets his arm
is thrown across her now

as she floats upward drawing him
out of deep tides crossing
their legs together all
the morning world comes floating in.

W. S.: The Tithon Sonnets

John Fuller

1. [*The Poet*]

Shall I then say that Eos cared for me,
Whitened my single window euery day
And with her beames lighted my poetry,
And willed the Terrors of the night away?
Heroes who fight long houres to earn their name
May claim a prompt inuigorating bed,
But those whose laboures seek a gradual fame
Despaire of joy vntil the night has fled,
When reason may resume, and the mind greet
The office of the sophist or the bard.
Thought is for them a solitarie feate.
The night is long, and all its minutes hard.
 Much more, then, am I welcome at her feast,
 One who from Night was drawn into her East.

1. Eos was a Titan of the Dawn (Aurora in Latin) who fell in love
with Tithonos and took him to Ethiopia. She asked Zeus to make him
immortal, but omitted to ask for eternal youth for him at the same time.
Tithonos, a brother of Priam, was a *rhapsode*, a performer of epic poetry.
There are no titles in the manuscript.

2. [*The Dawn*]

It is an Ethiopian maid who sings.
I hear and write down all her rhapsodies.
Yet after night's delightes, the morning brings
Loue's urgent whispers to his weeping knees.
I haue no passion now, if truth be told.
The light rebukes me. Dewe is on the lawn.
I wished to liue, but neuer to be old.
I am a shape abandoned by the Dawn.
O daughter of Hyperion, make clear
The dying of our nights, and of our daies.
Wake all the worlde, and travel far from here,
Far from an old man's bed and fruitlesse gaze.
    Let boys smile curses from their sweated sheetes,
    And tell the gods how much my heart still beates.

1. Compare Coleridge's 'Kubla Khan', line 39*ff.* ('It was an Abyssinian maid', &c). Coleridge had seen the manuscript of the Tithon Sonnets at Fakenham Hall in 1796, though he was the first to doubt Shakespeare's authorship.
9. i.e. Eos. Compare Ovid, *Amores*, 1.13, where Eos is eager to leave an old man's bed.

71

3. [*Memnon*]

I saw a creature hanging from a stemme,
Another leaping to a bending flow'r,
And had a quainte desire to be like them,
Without all knowledge of the changing hour,
Of the abrupt and euer-closing door
Of fatal illness, and aduance of rust,
Of the opposing army's sudden roar
At someone's darling lying in the dust.
Ah, Memnon, whom the tall Achilles slew,
That euer son should fall before his sire!
Now cloudes of starlings stirring in the blue,
Yearly recall smoke rising from his pyre.
　　And I am forced to watch each feathered ember
　　Mock, in its play, the babe that I remember.

9. Eos and Tithonos had two sons, Memnon and Emathion. For the
starlings, see Ovid, *Metamorphoses*, 13.717*ff*.

4. [*The Breath*]

Between my naturall disbelief in death
And knowledge that the world itselfe will cease:
Between the daring capture of a breath
And the large-minded risk of its release,
Stands my vncertain immortalite,
That steadie passage of the pretious air
Which is the gratefull planet's guarranty
Of ready and perpetuall repaire,
Breath after breath released in the conuiction
That my best future lies in the endeuour
To bide my time and to maintain the fiction
That in this moment I might liue for euer,

    Not in the accumulated past,
    But in each latest breath, not yet the last.

5. [*The Cricket*]

How may the gods take back the giftes they make?
It is the pleasure of rewardes to be
More for these giuers', than receiuers', sake,
Their miracles, their magnanimitie,
And for their tender care of all that dies,
And for their passing enuie of mere mortalls.
They moue in state across the changeless skies
To chase Time's wildings from their marble portals,
They grant men's mindeless wishes with a sigh,
They woo the beautie that they never had,
Which is short-liued, but tenderer thereby,
They clutche their hearts and know that they are sad.
   My cricket, tumbling from his blade of grass,
   Sings merrily of all that comes to pass.

13. In some versions of the story, Tithonos was turned into a cricket. Compare the first four lines of the third sonnet.

List of Contributors and Notes to Poems

Simon Armitage is Professor of Poetry at the University of Sheffield, was elected Professor of Poetry at Oxford University in 2015 and lives in West Yorkshire. His most recent collection is *Paper Aeroplane – Selected Poems 1989-2014*, drawing on twenty-five years of published work. In 2015 his play *The Last Days of Troy* was performed at Shakespeare's Globe, as were dramatized readings of his celebrated translation of *Sir Gawain and the Green Knight*. *Walking Home*, his prose account of his troubadour's journey along the Pennine Way, was a *Sunday Times* bestseller, and its companion volume, *Walking Away*, was published in 2015.

At school, Shakespeare's sonnets were usually presented as riddles rather than poems, things that had to be solved before they could be understood or enjoyed. For some they continue to be cryptogams, coded messages embedded with information about the poet's life, his religion, his authorship of the work and of course his sexuality, of which 'Sonnet 20' is often said to be the most revealing. I have pricked out my own coded sonnet in response.

Alan Brownjohn was born in London in 1931 and educated there and at Merton College, Oxford. His twelve individual volumes of verse are represented in his *Collected Poems* (2006) and *The Saner Places: Selected Poems* (2011). He is the author of four novels, of which *Windows on the Moon* (2009) is the most recent.

(1) adapts the theme of 'Sonnet 65', employing the manner and vocabulary of that sonnet and others in a slightly updated fashion.

John Burnside's latest collection of poetry is *All One Breath* (Jonathan Cape, 2014). His previous collection *Black Cat Bone* won the T. S. Eliot and Forward Prizes in 2011. He is Professor of Creative Writing at The University of St Andrews.

I have always been drawn to 'Sonnet 71', with its cool acceptance of mortality and, at the same time, its humane concern that the beloved will suffer grief after the speaker's death. It is a fact of all relationships, especially romantic love and, even more so, parenthood, that our own reconciliation with our mortality cannot be transferred to those we love: no matter how prepared we are for death, it does not ease the burden on the people we leave behind. As a parent, I am painfully aware of this fact: quite unafraid of death, (though not, perhaps, of the process of dying) I am, nevertheless, stricken by the fear of dying so soon that my children will suffer, both in practical terms and, of course, emotionally. If only my own acceptance of mortality could be communicated in full to those I care for – this is the central concern of the poem, 'Still Life', just as it lies at the core of 'Sonnet 71'.

My first impulse in responding to the sonnet was to echo the form; I soon gave up on that notion, partly because I wanted to respond to Shakespeare's work, not merely to echo it. So it was that, needing some other way of approaching the idea of 'the worm' that always shadows living, perishable things, I came in at an angle, via the European still life tradition, in which, it seemed to me, both ripeness and decay are celebrated (though in different ways) as part of the cycle of life. In a manner that cannot be paraphrased, it seemed to me that this tradition offers a notion – just as decay is implicit in ripeness, so regeneration is implicit in decay – that might soften the grief of the mourners, after a loved one's death.

Gillian Clarke has been National Poet of Wales since 2008. She was awarded the Queen's Gold Medal for Poetry 2010, and the Wilfred Owen Award in 2012. Her collection, *Ice,* was shortlisted for the T. S. Eliot Award 2012, and her poem-sequence, *The Gathering*, for the National Theatre of Wales, was performed on Snowdon in September 2014.

Wendy Cope worked as a primary school teacher until the publication of her first book of poems, *Making Cocoa for Kingsley*

Amis, in 1986. Since then she has been freelance and has published three more collections, most recently *Family Values* (2011). She has also written for children and edited several anthologies. A book of her prose pieces, entitled *Life, Love and The Archers,* appeared in 2014.

Kevin Crossley-Holland lives in north Norfolk. His most recent collection of poems, *The Breaking Hour,* was published by Enitharmon Press last summer. He is author of *The Penguin Book of Norse Myths,* translator of *Beowulf,* and a well-known Carnegie Medal-winning writer for children. President of the School Librarian Association 2012–16, he has been awarded Honorary Doctorates by Anglia Ruskin and Worcester, and is an Honorary Fellow of St. Edmund Hall, Oxford.

Imtiaz Dharker is a poet, artist and documentary film-maker. She was awarded the Queen's Gold Medal for Poetry in 2014 and is a recipient of the Cholmondley Award. Her collections include *Purdah* (Oxford University Press), *Postcards from God, I Speak for the Devil* and *The Terrorist at my Table* (all published by Penguin India and Bloodaxe Books UK), *Leaving Fingerprints* and *Over the Moon* (Bloodaxe Books UK).

This is such a perfect sonnet of absence and presence, presence in absence. The poem plays tricks on the mind with light and shade, with words that look and sound the same but make cunning grammatical shifts. It takes reality and tilts it into the dream where the lover comes. Longing like this is close to grief.

Carol Ann Duffy lives in Manchester, where she is Professor and Creative Director of the Writing School at Manchester Metropolitan University. She has written for both children and adults, and her poetry has received many awards, including the Signal Prize for Children's Verse, the Whitbread, Forward and T. S. Eliot Prizes, and the Lannan and E. M. Forster Prize in America. She was appointed Poet Laureate in 2009. In 2011 *The Bees* won the Costa Poetry Award, and in 2012 she won the PEN Pinter Prize.

Douglas Dunn was born in 1942. He has published ten collections of poems, as well as *New Selected Poems* (Faber & Faber, 2003) and, more recently, *A Line in the Water*, with etchings by Norman Ackroyd (Royal Academy, 2009), and a chapbook *Invisible Ink* (Mariscat, 2011). He received an OBE in 2003, and the Queen's Gold Medal for poetry in 2013. He retired as Professor of English at the University of St Andrews in 2008.

Paul Farley was born in Liverpool in 1965 and studied at the Chelsea School of Art. He has published four books of poetry with Picador, including most recently *The Dark Film* (2012). He has also written widely for radio, as well as publishing several non-fiction titles, and has edited a selection of John Clare's poetry. He has received numerous awards including *Sunday Times* Young Writer of the Year, the Whitbread Poetry Prize and the E. M. Forster Award from the American Academy of Arts & Letters. He also presents BBC Radio 4's contemporary poetry programme The Echo Chamber.

Elaine Feinstein has been publishing poems for half a century and has received many awards. She has travelled across the world to read her poems, which have been translated into most European languages. She has also written prize-winning novels and five biographies. Her versions of the poetry of Marina Tsvetaeva, a *New York Times* Book of the Year, have remained in print since 1971. She has served on the Council of the Royal Society of Literature as a judge for most of the current literary prizes, and as Chair of the Judges for the T. S. Eliot Award. Her most recent book of poems, *Portraits*, came out from Carcanet in February 2015.

> As to my choice of sonnet: lines from Shakespeare's noble 'Sonnet 116' have remained with me all my life. Some time ago, however, a painful marital tangle led me to question the virtues of such a commitment. The poem rises now out of the ambiguities I came to understand.

John Fuller is a poet, novelist and critic. He is an Emeritus Fellow of Magdalen College, Oxford, where, from 1966 to 2002, he was Tutor in English. The first of his seven novels, *Flying to Nowhere*, won a Whitbread Prize and was shortlisted for the Booker Prize. He is the editor of the Clarendon Press edition of the plays of John Gay, author of *W. H. Auden: a commentary*, and editor of *The Oxford Book of Sonnets*. He has published collections of short stories, anthologies, texts for composers, and works for children. Among his most recent books are *Who is Ozymandias? and other Puzzles in Poetry* (Chatto and

Windus, 2011), *New Selected Poems 1983–2008* (Chatto, 2012) and *Gravel in my Shoe* (Chatto, 2015).

David Harsent has published eleven volumes of poetry. *Legion* won the Forward Prize for best collection in 2005; *Night* (2011) won the Griffin International Poetry Prize. *In Secret*, his English versions of poems by Yannis Ritsos, was published in 2102 in the UK and in the USA in 2013. His most recent collection, *Fire Songs* (2014) won the T. S. Eliot Prize. He has collaborated with composers – most often with Harrison Birtwistle – on commissions that have been performed at (among other venues) the Royal Opera House, the Royal Albert Hall (Proms), the Wigmore Hall, the Concertgebouw, the Wales Millennium Centre, The Megaron (Athens), the South Bank Centre, the Edinburgh Festival, the Aldeburgh Festival, the Salzburg Festival and Carnegie Hall. He is Professor of Creative Writing at the University of Roehampton.

Alan Jenkins was born in 1955 and has lived for most of his life in London. His collections of poetry include, most recently, *A Shorter Life* (2005), *Revenants* (2013) and *Marine* (with John Kinsella, 2015). He is Deputy Editor and Poetry Editor of the *Times Literary Supplement*. For some years he part-owned and crewed a small, all-wooden sailing vessel.

P. J. Kavanagh has published novels, essays and poems, including *Collected Poems* in 1992 and *New Selected Poems* in 2014, both by Carcanet.

I think that we often underestimate our own humanity, and art can give it a necessary and deserved glow. Leopardi's miseries, Yeats's exaltations, these 'exaggerations' of art can help us. Shakespeare uses the word 'more' twice in one line and he hints at poetic 'survival' in 'Sonnet 18' ('Shall I compare thee…').

As I believe that poems should arrive involuntarily – however formalised the final expression – the main body of my attempt is an unaltered narrative of a dream, because dreams sometimes leave behind them this 'glow'.

Jackie Kay is the author of *Red Dust Road*, her memoir about her search for her birth parents and the story of her adoptive ones. She is currently Chancellor of the University of Salford and Professor of Creative Writing at the University of Newcastle. Her most recent book of poetry is *Fiere*, shortlisted for the Costa Award and published by Picador.

Mimi Khalvati has published eight collections with Carcanet Press, including *The Meanest Flower*, shortlisted for the T. S. Eliot Prize, and *Child: New and Selected Poems 1991–2011*, a Poetry Book Society Special Commendation. Her most recent, *The Weather Wheel*, is a Poetry Book Society Recommendation and was a Book of the Year 2014 in *The Independent*.

'Sonnet 33' seemed to connect in my mind with two – possibly related – projects I had been mulling over: writing poems about the sun, and writing poems about my son, who was diagnosed with schizophrenia when he was 26. Given the stigma attached to this illness and the inevitable misconceptions we hold, I've often felt the urge to try and write more about my son's experience of it, but from a mother's point of view.

Nick Laird was born in County Tyrone in 1975. He worked for many years as a litigator in London and Warsaw, and now lives in New York, where he teaches at Princeton and NYU. He has won many awards for his fiction and poetry, including the Betty Trask Prize, the Geoffrey Faber Memorial Prize, the Somerset Maugham Award and the Rooney Prize for Irish Literature.

For a starting point I took 'Sonnet 38', especially the line is 'How can my Muse want subject to invent / While thou dost breathe'. My version imagines all the dead sonneteers (who were, historically, male) being resurrected and press-ganged into writing something equal to the speaker's love, meaning both the (female) beloved, and, I suppose, the state of being in love – and the failure of those attempts. I wanted the conceit to try to catch something of the competitive air and gamesmanship of the sonnets.

Michael Longley has published ten collections of poetry, the most recent being *The Stairwell* (2014).

'The Sonnets' is partly a response to Shakespeare's 'Sonnet 55'. I wrote it in December 2014, just in time to mark the centenary of the beginning of the Great War. Shakespeare would have been packed into many a young soldier's kitbag. He served (and continues to serve) on all the fronts.

Roger McGough CBE, FRSL, is President of the Poetry Society, a Freeman of the City of Liverpool and presenter of Poetry Please on BBC Radio 4.

> Dear Mr Shakespeare, (or Will, if I may),
> All my attempts to compose a sonnet in your honour failed, so taking 14 opening lines from your corpus, I assembled them to reflect my own inadequacy.
> Yours, in gratitude,
> Roger

Andrew Motion was Poet Laureate from 1999–2009. His latest collection of poems is *Peace Talks* (2015).

> The more often I re-read Shakespeare's sonnets, and the deeper I fell into their world, the more strongly I felt attracted by their onward-driving but fast-and-loose way with narrative. This is why I've chosen to respond to several sonnets, and to create what I hope is a sympathetic structure of my own. A story made of emotional statements. Stations of the heart.

Paul Muldoon is the author of twelve books of poetry, including *One Thousand Things Worth Knowing* (2015).

> The area of north Armagh where I was brought up is renowned for apple growing. Though apples were grown in Ireland long before the Plantation, the fact that English planters were required to grow them accounts substantially

for the prevalence of the fruit. I chose 'Sonnet 15' as a stock for my own little scion because its key image is itself drawn from the art of grafting.

Sean O'Brien is Professor of Creative Writing at Newcastle University. His eighth collection of poems, *The Beautiful Librarians*, appeared in 2015 and was a Poetry Book Society Choice. His *Collected Poems* was published in 2012. He has received the T. S. Eliot Prize, the E. M. Forster Award, the Somerset Maugham Award, the Forward Prize (three times) and the Roehampton Poetry Prize. His translation of Dante's *Inferno* appeared in 2006. His work for the stage includes a verse translation of Aristophanes' *The Birds* for the National Theatre, *Keepers of the Flame* for the RSC/Live Theatre, and a verse translation of Tirso de Molina's *Don Gil of the Green Breeches* (Ustinov Studio/Arcola). His critical work includes *The Deregulated Muse* (1998) and *Journeys to the Interior: Ideas of England in Contemporary Poetry* (2012). His novel *Afterlife* appeared in 2009 and its successor is in preparation. He writes for *The Guardian*, *The Independent* and the *Times Literary Supplement*.

'Sonnet 94' addresses a temperament which seems inscrutably attractive, drawing attention while remaining unresponsive. The poem diagnoses at least the threat of corruption arising from this impassive vanity, and I wanted to explore this territory.

Bernard O'Donoghue was born in County Cork in 1945. Since 1965 he has lived in Oxford where he is now an Emeritus

Fellow in English of Wadham College. His *Selected Poems* was published by Faber in 2008.

> The dodginess of my poem is in response to what I think is the dubious undercurrent in 'Sonnet 49'. Though Shakespeare's narrator pretends to be abdicating any rights on his own part (even raising his legal hand against himself), the line that stays in the mind at the end is 'Within the knowledge of mine own desert'. There is a veiled, sinister self-righteousness behind it all. And it is often so in life: a passive aggression that isn't really passive.

Ruth Padel's ninth collection, shortlisted for the T. S. Eliot Prize, was *Learning to Make an Oud in Nazareth*, a meditation on craftsmanship, history and the Middle East. She is Poetry Fellow at King's London, where she teaches Creative Writing, but began as a Greek scholar. Her prose work includes books on Greek tragedy and the influence of Greek myth on rock music, three much-loved books about reading poetry, and a first-hand exploration of tiger conservation. She is also a Trustee of the Zoological Society of London and New Networks for Nature. Her collection *Darwin – A Life in Poems* was turned into a play by the Mephisto Theatre Company in Galway, and her selected poems have been published in Polish under the title *The Art of Kintsugi*. Her awards include a Cholmondeley Award, First Prize in the National Poetry Competition and a British Council Darwin Now award for her novel *Where the Serpent Lives* on wildlife conservation.

The metaphors in 'Sonnet 60' melt into each other like waves. I took from them the idea of life as a wave that starts at sea and ends on the shore, and then asked that metaphor to turn itself on its head. I was helped by the structure. A sonnet is eight and six but the key word *Time* seems to cut 'Sonnet 60' in two equal halves and then has all the action. That word arrives after seven lines, and is the subject of some increasingly sinister verbs: it *transfixes*, *delves*, *feeds* and operates Death's *scythe;* its *hand* ends the poem. I found myself resisting it, and working instead towards a flowing poem, which reverses the metaphor underling 'Sonnet 60'.

Don Paterson was born in Dundee in 1963. He is the author of *Nil Nil* (1993), winner of the Forward Prize for Best First Collection; *God's Gift to Women* (1997), winner of both the T. S. Eliot Prize and the Geoffrey Faber Memorial Prize; and *Landing Light* (2003), which won both the T. S. Eliot Prize and the Whitbread Prize for Poetry. *Rain*, his most recent collection, won the Forward Prize for Best Collection in 2009, the same year that he was awarded the Queen's Gold Medal for Poetry. He has also published versions of Antonio Machado (*The Eyes*, 1999) and Rainer Maria Rilke (*Orpheus*, 2006), as well as two collections of aphorisms. His *Selected Poems* appeared in 2012.

Michael Symmons Roberts was born in Preston, Lancashire in 1963. His sixth poetry collection, *Drysalter* (2013), won the Forward Prize and the Costa Poetry Award. His fourth collection, *Corpus* (2004), won the Whitbread Prize for Poetry and was shortlisted for the Griffin International Poetry Prize. He is an award-winning broadcaster, and his work as a librettist (mainly with composer James MacMillan) has been performed in venues across the world. Their 2007 opera, *The Sacrifice*, won the Royal Philharmonic Society Award for Opera. He has also published novels and non-fiction, and is Professor of Poetry at Manchester Metropolitan University. His Selected Poems is forthcoming this year.

Robin Robertson is from the north-east coast of Scotland. He has published five collections of poetry and received a number of accolades, including the Petrarca Preis, the E. M. Forster Award from the American Academy of Arts and Letters, and Forward Prizes in all three categories. His selected poems, *Sailing the Forest*, was published recently.

Fiona Sampson has been published in more than thirty languages. She has received the Newdigate Prize, the Zlaten Prsten (Macedonia), the Charles Angoff Award (US), a Cholmondeley Award, and awards from the Poetry Book Society, Arts Council England and Wales, and the Society of Authors. She has also been shortlisted twice for both T. S. Eliot and Forward Prizes.

Jo Shapcott was born in London. Poems from her three award-winning collections, *Electroplating the Baby* (1988), *Phrase Book* (1992) and *My Life Asleep* (1998) are gathered as selected poems in *Her Book* (2000). She has won a number of literary prizes including the Commonwealth Writers' Prize for Best

First Collection, the Forward Prize for Best Collection and the National Poetry Competition (twice). *Tender Taxes*, her versions of Rilke, was published in 2001. Her most recent collection, *Of Mutability*, was published in 2010 and won the Costa Book Award. In 2011 Jo Shapcott was awarded the Queen's Gold Medal for Poetry.

'Sonnet 73' lodged itself in my imagination the first time I read it, in my teens. I remember being stunned by the second line for the way it corrects and revisits itself, the way it looks, and looks again, and looks a third time at leaves on a branch (some leaves, then few, then none), correcting and revising as it goes. The line speeds up time so that we watch a whole life cycle coming to its close in ten syllables. My poem bows to the original somewhere in every line and spins round it in grateful celebration.

The Poetry Archive

Recordings of 10 of the new poems and their corresponding Shakespeare sonnets can be found on the Poetry Archive website at www.poetryarchive.org/shakespeare400

Alternatively, you can access these recordings using the QR codes below. To use these QR codes, you need to download a QR scanner onto your smartphone or tablet. Scan the codes in this book with your scanner, and the poem page on the Poetry Archive website will open (as long as you have Internet access). Click the play button to listen. These recordings are also available to buy in the Poetry Archive downloads store if you would like to save them and listen to them offline.

Alan Brownjohn – A Winter Elegy

Alan Brownjohn – A Call

Gillian Clarke – Magnetism

Imtiaz Dharker – The Trick

Jackie Kay – Thirty-Five

Mimi Khalvati – Hearing Voices

Andrew Motion – Rhapsodies

Bernard O'Donoghue – At the Hallé

Don Paterson – Two

Fiona Sampson – Drowned Man

Jo Shapcott – 2014/2015

Index of Poets

Index of First Lines